P9-DBT-163

Hillary Rodham Clinton
dreams taking flight

Kathleen Krull

Illustrated by Amy June Bates

Simon & Schuster Books for Young Readers

New York   London   Toronto   Sydney

Once there was a girl who wanted to fly. She dreamed of zooming in a spaceship up through the clouds into outer space, learning new things about Earth.

She wrote to the national space agency to volunteer. But it was 1961, and some paths were still closed to women, such as the job of astronaut.

Take a deep breath, look ahead, and keep trying to fly.

Even when she was little, she wanted to do something big and fearless. In different ways her mom and dad encouraged her to chase after her dreams, to soar.

Stand up for yourself, and keep your balance.

For someone who loved to learn, school was a big adventure. By eighth grade she could talk and argue about current stories in the news.

8

Even if you make a mistake, never be afraid to show your intelligence.

9

Shaking the hand of Martin Luther King Jr. was
something she would never forget. He inspired her,
more than anyone, to look for ways to help other people.

Find heroes to
lift you up.

11

She liked to lead. In high school she was elected vice president of her junior class. But when she ran for president, she lost. One of the boys she ran against said she was "really stupid if she thought a girl could be elected president."

When borders surround you, try to break through.

Try harder—
you can do better.

When borders surround you, try to break through.

She darted off to an all-women's college, where
she started learning how our government works.
A job in government was looking like the best way
for her to help people.

She was the first student to speak at her college's
graduation ceremony—a big and fearless speech
that kept people clapping for seven minutes.

You don't have time for fear.

15

Try harder—
you can do better.

She decided to apply to law school. A lawyer really could change the world—or at least the lives of the neediest people, by making the laws work for them.

A professor at one law school told her, "We don't need any more women." She chose another school.

Who are the people who need our help
the most? Children who are poor, neglected,
abused. She launched her career as a lawyer
to make these children's lives better.

Dare to compete.

When she became the First Lady of one of the poorest states, people noticed that she was always on the go, getting things done, using politics as a way to help people.

Some people wondered how much her career would take flight. Others mocked her looks and wished she would just stay home.

Think of the world as bigger than yourself, and carry on.

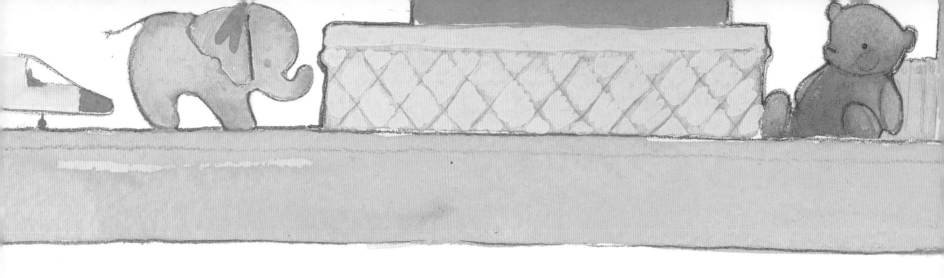

She gave birth to her own daughter
and began whispering encouragement.

You can be anything you want—
even an astronaut.

Her husband ran for United States president.
He said voters would get "two for the price of one,"
referring to his smart wife. This shocked some people.

Be who you are,
get through it,
and wait for times to change.

In her eight years in the White House, she was a new kind of First Lady, blasting off like a rocket. She tried to cover a lot of ground, and not everything she did was a success.

When something makes you fall,
rise up again.

"Every woman in public life needs to develop

skin as tough as rhinoceros hide."
—Eleanor Roosevelt

She flew into advancing the rights of women around the world. Always she was in the public eye, with no privacy.

On days when people criticized her no matter what she did, she asked herself how her biggest hero, Eleanor Roosevelt, would have coped.

Take the lead role in your own life.

There were only one hundred senators. Each one truly could make a difference in the areas they cared about the most. She ran for senator, won, and went airborne in politics by herself for the first time.

Take a risk, and dare to change the world.

Bit by bit she sailed up through the clouds. Not afraid to fly, daring to compete, she decided to run for the highest office in the land. Was the land ready? No matter—she was propelling her way into history. Making a difference.

Sooner or later, we will have a woman president, and it will be because of every girl who has wanted to fly.

Three—two—one—liftoff!

(Pages 4–5) HILLARY RODHAM was born on October 26, 1947, and grew up in Park Ridge, Illinois, a town near the new O'Hare International Airport. Her first career goal was to be an astronaut. She and her little brother Hugh played astronaut games in their basement, with her at the controls of a spaceship whizzing to Mars.

When Hillary was fourteen, she learned about the National Aeronautics and Space Administration. Established three years earlier in 1958, NASA was one of President John F. Kennedy's favorite programs. She fired off a letter to NASA asking for help. What should she do to prepare? NASA wrote back: There was no such thing as a woman astronaut. No girls allowed.

Hillary felt deflated by the rejection, though later she realized that her severe nearsightedness would have disqualified her anyway. NASA started accepting women in 1978. That year Sally Ride was able to join, and in 1983, Ride became the first American woman in space.

(Pages 6–7) When Hillary was four, a neighborhood bully named Suzy often picked on her. Finally her mother told her to fight back, to stand up for herself. So she did. Suzy never bothered her again.

Hillary's mother, who could remember a time when women couldn't yet vote, always pushed Hillary to think just as big as her two brothers. Did Hillary want to be the first woman judge on the Supreme Court? She liked astronaut better.

Hillary's father, a former navy officer, taught her to play baseball and football. Hitting a baseball was her weakness. So he spent hours pitching to her, over and over, until she finally learned how to hit the ball with a satisfying *crack*. She became a good athlete, though there were no sports teams for girls then.

Hillary's father had strong opinions that most people didn't dare question—but in talking to him she learned how to argue.

(Pages 8–9) Hillary was never afraid to express herself and voice her opinions. She always did it, even though she grew up at a time when girls were often hesitant to show their intelligence for fear that boys wouldn't like them.

Besides bringing home straight-A report cards, Hillary took lessons in piano and ballet and swimming. As a Girl Scout she racked up one merit badge after another. She raised money for the children of Mexican workers who picked fruits and vegetables on the local farms. She went from door to door in support of the presidential candidate she liked.

Unlike most kids her age, Hillary spoke in complete sentences, even paragraphs. Teachers encouraged her. Her history teacher in high school organized a mock presidential debate during the national election—and picked Hillary to play one of the candidates because she loved to argue and debate so much.

(Pages 10–11) One night the minister from Hillary's Methodist church took her and other young people to see Martin Luther King Jr., the civil rights leader urging equal rights for African Americans. Hillary loved his speech—especially his message of nonviolence and working within the system. She never changed her mind that racial injustice was the biggest problem in America. Most of her later work with children was a way to address this.

(Pages 12–13) Hillary and others didn't have many women in public life to look to as role models. One of her heroes and one of the few women in politics then was Margaret Chase Smith, a senator from Maine from 1949 to 1972. In fiction one of Hillary's heroes was *Little Women*'s Jo March, who supported her entire family with her writing.

Hillary was always up for challenges and came to be known as fearless. Once, a boy she liked challenged her to ride his skateboard. When she successfully navigated a hill, he agreed to take her to senior prom.

In 1965, Hillary graduated from Maine South High School in the top 5 percent of her class. She was voted Girl Most Likely to Succeed, despite losing the election for student-body president.

Her newest career goal, lasting into her late teens, was to become a doctor, since medicine was a field opening up to women. It sounded like a huge way of helping others, except for that little problem she had with getting sick at the sight of blood.

(Pages 14–15) The prestigious Ivy League schools—such as Yale, Harvard, Brown, and Columbia—were still closed to women. Hillary chose Wellesley College in Massachusetts, one of the illustrious Seven Sisters women's colleges, because she felt she could take more risks without boys around.

During Hillary's freshman year the National Organization for Women was founded, fighting for equal opportunities for women.

In her junior year she was elected student-body president, wearing a style of glasses that aviators wear while flying planes. Deeply sorrowed by the death of Martin Luther King Jr., she joined a peaceful demonstration, organized a student strike, and worked to recruit more black students and faculty.

Like many students at the time, Hillary strongly opposed the Vietnam War. In the 1968 presidential election she supported the antiwar nominee. She was at the famous protest at the Democratic National Convention in Chicago, but was horrified by the violence, which she didn't see as a solution to problems.

That summer she served as an intern in Washington, D.C., to see the workings of politics firsthand.

At Hillary's graduation in 1969, as president of the student government, she delivered a speech that made some consider her a spokesperson for her generation. She was critical of President Richard Nixon, as well as of her fellow speaker, a senator. "We feel that for too long our leaders have used politics as the art of the possible," she said. "The challenge now is to practice politics as the art of making what appears to be impossible, possible. . . . We are, all of us, exploring a world that none of us understands and attempting to create within that uncertainty." *Life* magazine named her one of the brightest student leaders in America, and she appeared on TV talk shows.

(Pages 16–17) In 1969 at Yale Law School, Hillary was one of 27 women in a class of 237—law was still a new field for women. Most professors were skeptical about women becoming lawyers, and ten of the twenty-seven women dropped out before graduating. (Harvard was the school with "too many" women.)

In 1971, Hillary fell in love with fellow Yale law student Bill Clinton: "No one understands me better and no one can make me laugh the way Bill does," she said.

By 1972, with more women entering politics, some were predicting that Hillary would be the first woman president. She took a summer job with an antipoverty organization in Washington, for no pay, and applied for a grant that allowed her to live there. She met Marian Wright Edelman, who had gone from Yale Law School to become the first black woman lawyer in Mississippi. Edelman founded the Children's Defense Fund, a groundbreaking group that helps poor and minority children get basic services, and became Hillary's most important mentor.

Hillary decided children's rights was going to be her focus. Her first published paper was "Children Under the Law," about abused and neglected children. Child abuse was a brand-new field—in her classes at the Yale Child Study Center she was one of the first to study the subject.

(Pages 18–19) After law school Hillary's first job was as a lawyer for the Children's Defense Fund. "I want to be a voice for America's children," she said.

Her reputation growing, she was asked to join the staff of the committee investigating criminal charges against Richard Nixon relating to the Watergate scandal. One of three women in the group of forty-four, she became part of history as Nixon resigned in 1974.

By then some were whispering that this twenty-six-year-old woman was *amazing*.

After marrying Bill in 1975, Hillary was a professor at the University of Arkansas School of Law. Then she became the first woman lawyer at the largest firm in the state, where she earned far more money than her husband. She took on many cases for free, especially those that involved the protection of children. Twice she was hailed as one of the hundred most influential lawyers in America.

(Pages 20–21) Hillary worked behind the scenes to help Bill get elected governor. When he won, she became the First Lady of Arkansas.

While working at the law firm and becoming its first female partner (part owner), Hillary also headed a committee to improve the quality of education in Arkansas, which had a low ranking compared to other states. She worked on several other committees that helped children and families.

President Jimmy Carter appointed her to head the board of directors of the Legal Services Corporation, which offers legal help to those who can't afford a lawyer. She also headed the American Bar Association's Commission on Women in the Profession. The commission examined the considerable bias against women lawyers, including the "glass ceiling" that seemed to prevent women from getting the best jobs, and got the ABA to adopt measures to combat this bias.

(Pages 22–23) At Hillary's law firm there was no such thing as maternity leave. She convinced the firm to give her a four-month leave after Chelsea was born in 1980. Hillary was part of a new generation of women balancing family with career. She was named Arkansas Woman of the Year in 1983 and Arkansas Mother of the Year in 1984.

One of Chelsea's early career goals was to be an astronaut—just like her mother. She dreamed of building colonies in space, and at thirteen she attended the United States Space Camp in Alabama. Her current job is as a business analyst specializing in health care.

(Pages 24–25) During the 1992 election Hillary managed Bill's campaign and worked eighteen-hour days to get him elected. She became a magnet for controversy as the first First Lady to hold advanced degrees and to have her own thriving career. Until that point most First Ladies had busied themselves with just about anything other than politics. Many people agreed with former President Richard Nixon, who said a president needed "a wife who's intelligent, but not too intelligent."

(Pages 26–27) Right away Hillary set up her office in the West Wing of the White House, the president's space, instead of in the East Wing, where First Ladies usually stayed. It was a sign that her work as one of his major policy advisers was important too. She took part in as many as thirty meetings a day.

President Clinton appointed Hillary to head the Task Force on National Health Care Reform, overseeing the work of five hundred people. President Clinton and Hillary agreed that the health care crisis was the most important problem to solve. Hillary crafted a gigantic plan to provide health care for every person in America, even the thirty-seven million adults and children who had no health insurance at all. She became the first First Lady to make government policy and introduce major legislation to Congress.

Her plan was so fiercely opposed that she had to start wearing a bulletproof vest while on a bus tour to rally support for it. The plan was dropped in 1994 without Congress ever voting on it. It failed for several reasons, one of which was that so many people found Hillary's ambitions and independence upsetting. A poll at the time showed that 68 percent believed that a First Lady should not even be attending a president's policy meetings.

(Pages 28–29) This quote is one of many famous pieces of wisdom from Eleanor Roosevelt. Before moving to the White House, Hillary read forty-three books about the lives of the previous First Ladies.

She admired Dolley Madison, Patricia Nixon, and Lady Bird Johnson, as well as Jacqueline Kennedy, who met with her many times to give advice. But her biggest hero was Roosevelt, another trailblazer accused of meddling in government, someone who received stacks of hate mail. Roosevelt learned to deal with the criticism by refusing to take it personally and developing a tougher skin.

After 1994, Hillary lowered her profile but worked as hard as ever. Our most-traveled First Lady, she visited more than eighty countries, mostly on behalf of women's rights. At the Fourth World Conference on Women in Beijing, she made a moving, influential speech against inhumane practices toward women in China and around the world: "If women are healthy and educated, their families will flourish. . . . And when families flourish, communities and nations will flourish." She won numerous awards from other countries for her work on behalf of women.

Of all her accomplishments as First Lady, Hillary was proudest of 1997's Adoption and Safe Families Act, which streamlined the foster care system; within five years the number of children moving from foster care to permanent homes more than doubled. She also helped establish the State Children's Health Insurance Program, helped create the Office on Violence Against Women, and hosted numerous White House conferences on children's issues.

(Pages 30–31) One of the hardest decisions Hillary ever made was to compete in politics on her own. In 2000, after becoming the first American First Lady to run for public office, she was elected to the United States Senate. She was the first female senator from New York and received 55 percent of the vote. (She wore her trademark pantsuits on the Senate floor. Only since 1993 have women been allowed to wear pants in the Senate.)

Hillary served on five Senate committees, including the Committee on Armed Services, through which she supported military action in Afghanistan in order to combat terrorism while improving the lives of Afghan women. After the September 11, 2001, attack on New York City, she helped wherever she could, especially in organizing aid to the ten thousand children who lost a parent in the attack. In 2002 she was one of seventy-seven senators to authorize President George W. Bush's decision to take military action in Iraq.

In 2002 and 2003, Hillary was voted Most Admired Woman in the United States in the Gallup Poll.

She won reelection in 2006 with 67 percent of the vote.

In 2007, Hillary announced she would run for president, something so big and so fearless it seemed impossible—even to her. Once she said, "Running for president is like pitching a no-hitter."

In all of American history, no woman has ever been president of the United States. Hillary Clinton has soared higher than any other American woman who has tried. The ones who went before her are: Victoria Woodhull (1872), Belva Lockwood (1884 and 1888), Whitney Slocomb (1960), Margaret Chase Smith (1964), Charlene Mitchell (1968), Shirley Chisholm (1972), Linda Jenness (1972), Evelyn Reed (1972), Bella Abzug (1972), Patsy Mink (1972), Margaret Wright (1976), Ellen McCormack (1976 and 1980), Deirdre Griswold (1980), Maureen Smith (1980), Sonia Johnson (1984), Gavrille Holmes (1984), Isabell Masters (1984, 1992, 1996, 2000, and 2004), Patricia Schroeder (1988), Willa Kenoyer (1988), Lenora Fulani (1988 and 1992), Gloria La Riva (1992), Helen Halyard (1992), Marsha Feinland (1996), Mary Hollis (1996), Diane Templin (1996), Monica Moorehead (1996 and 2000), Elizabeth Dole (2000), Cathy Brown (2000), and Carol Moseley Braun (2004).

★ *Sources* ★

Bernstein, Carl. *A Woman in Charge: The Life of Hillary Rodham Clinton*. New York: Knopf, 2007.

Clinton, Hillary Rodham. *It Takes a Village: And Other Lessons Children Teach Us*. New York: Simon & Schuster, 1996.

———. *Living History*. New York: Simon & Schuster, 2003.

* Guernsey, JoAnn Bren. *Hillary Rodham Clinton*. Minneapolis: Lerner, 2005.

* Gullo, Jim. *The Importance of Hillary Rodham Clinton*. San Diego: Lucent, 2004.

* Kozar, Richard. *Hillary Rodham Clinton*. Philadelphia: Chelsea House, 1998.

Maraniss, David. *First in His Class: A Biography of Bill Clinton*. New York: Simon & Schuster, 1995.

* Ryan, Bernard Jr. *Hillary Rodham Clinton: First Lady and Senator*. New York: Ferguson, 2004.

* Sherrow, Victoria. *Hillary Rodham Clinton*. New York: Dillon, 1993.

* Thimmesh, Catherine. *Madam President: The Extraordinary, True (and Evolving) Story of Women in Politics*, revised edition. Boston: Houghton Mifflin, 2008.

* FOR YOUNG READERS